To Begin the World Over Again

Kevin Osborne

and

Alex Bleier

info@thomaspaineinstitute.com

CONTENTS

To Begin the World Over Again

*To the intellectual giants who began
the world over again in America three
centuries ago, and to Ayn Rand who
has given us the philosophy to begin
over again—again—in today's world
and this time make it last.*

To Begin the World Over Again

Abstract. In January 1776 a British-born firebrand by the name of Thomas Paine proclaimed in his pamphlet "Common Sense" that "We have it in our power to begin the world over again." Up until then, no prediction had ever come close to the optimism of that vision.

Paine was referring to a new nation, one that was to become the United States of America. It would be the first in history founded on the Enlightenment principle of individual rights. To secure those rights, America's founders, imbued with the spirit of its Declaration of Independence, designed a constitution to minimize initiated physical coercion in human affairs. And equally important, it was a constitution that looked to limit America's government to a single function, to protect its citizens from those who would practice that evil.

Armed—charged—with such a constitution, America, in its first century and a half, grew and flourished at a rate and to an extent never before seen. America was the freest and most prosperous nation in history. Long has it stood as a beacon of freedom to the world's oppressed. America in the late 18th century truly did begin the world over again, her rise was that extraordinary.

But the beacon has dimmed.

What conditions existed in 1776 America to convince Thomas Paine that America had the power to begin the world over again? How did its constitution drive America's rise? Why is she now in decline, though still a great power? Is a permanently free sovereign state even possible today, or is it too late?

This essay explores these questions and answers "No" to the last. It is not too late.

The Authors: The authors have produced two works that are prequels to the vision advanced in this essay: the 2014 nonfiction book, *The Prometheus Connection*, and the 2021 novel, *The Prometheus Frontier*. **Kevin Osborne** holds a PhD in Philosophy from the City University of New York, and serves as the principal author and the lead member of the Philosophy Team. **Alex Bleier**, with degrees in Math, Philosophy, and Technical Communication has an extensive career in computer consulting, spanning the gamut from Fortune 500 companies to Silicon Valley startups and now to the newly formed Thomas Paine Institute, as Executive Director.

THE NECESSARY CONDITIONS

We want first to answer this question: What conditions existed in 1776 America to convince Paine that America had it in its power to begin the world over again? He states in "Common Sense" that "In [these] pages I offer nothing more than simple facts, plain arguments, and common sense."[1]

Evidently, for Paine it bordered on the self-evident. Simple facts, plain arguments, common sense reveal that the following conditions, already existing in America, gave her the power to which he was referring.

Real Estate

In the case of Real Estate, it was the "simple fact" that the thirteen original colonies were spread over nearly half a million square miles. Paine knew that the colonies, by defeating Britain, would be in a position to gain sovereign control of that land. Through the 1788 Treaty of Paris, that is exactly what happened: the thirteen original colonies officially became the United States of America.

Defense Capability

The colonies had defense capability. As Paine pointed out, in what seems to be a certain amount of hyperbole, the colonies taken as a whole have "the largest body of armed and disciplined men of any power under Heaven." It had allies from France, Spain, and the Netherlands. Regarding naval power, he states "no country on the globe is so happily situated, or so internally capable of raising a fleet as America. Tar, timber, iron, and cordage are her natural produce. We need go abroad for nothing."[2]

Fiscal and Human Resources

The colonies had potential fiscal resources from taxes, bonds, foreign loans. As Paine puts it, "Debts we have none."[3]

For Human Resources, the colonies, lit as they were by the Enlightenment reverence for reason, learning, and freedom, had largely literate populations. These were populations which gave birth to the intellectual giants known as America's Founding Fathers.

Philosophy

Most importantly, Paine knew the colonists, imbued with the Enlightenment spirit, possessed the philosophic principles to justify casting off the oppressive yoke of the British Crown. At the end of "Common Sense," he galvanized the colonists to action when he declared "nothing can settle our affairs [grievances with Britain] so expeditiously as an open and determined Declaration of Independence."[4]

Thomas Jefferson rose to that challenge within months, with America's Declaration of Independence advancing a philosophic principle which was to become immortal. This is the principle of the unalienable right to Life, Liberty, and the pursuit of Happiness. Paine knew that the colonists had the philosophy to begin the world over again. History proved him right.[5]

AMERICA'S RISE

Immediately after winning independence, America's survival was less than certain. Its economy was a primitive agrarian one, dependent on manufactured imports, and supported by a meager population of barely three million (one third that of England).

This is not to say the new nation was without strengths. It had abundant though untapped natural resources and a population that doubled every twenty years, the fastest rate in the world. It was also a population that, though lacking higher education, was largely literate. And even more importantly, it was, as Hezekiah Niles, a publisher of the time noted, a population imbued with "a universal ambition to go forward" reflecting the optimistic Enlightenment mindset of the age.

Scholars point out that America's founders framed a basically laissez-faire constitution to capitalize on and protect these strengths. ***Article One Section Eight*** restricted the government's ability to intervene in the marketplace. ***Sections Eight and Ten*** established sound currency. ***Section Nine*** prohibited states from erecting trade barriers. ***Amendment Five*** protected private property.[6]

A Revolutionary Patent System

Not always remembered, yet vital for jumpstarting America's nascent economy, were words in ***Article One Section Eight*** giving Congress the power to "promote the Progress of Science and useful Arts, by securing for limited Times to Authors and Inventors the exclusive Right to their respective Writings and Discoveries." This simple statement was revolutionary. It was the first time the constitution of any nation included an intellectual property clause.[7]

How did this happen? To put it simply, the Founders, in their wisdom, studied the history of patents and learned what *not* to do. They looked to the patent system of England, the country then leading the Industrial Revolution, and found it wanting. Laws limited the ability of inventors to sell or license the rights to their inventions. Patent application fees were very high. This meant only the very wealthy had the capital to commercialize their inventions.[8]

The framers of America's patent system wanted to avoid such limitations. They wanted a patent system that would unleash the entrepreneurial energy of ordinary people.[9] The 1787-1788 constitution and the laws promulgated from it accomplished exactly that.

In contrast to England, America's patent system was exceedingly friendly to inventors. It explicitly included provisions designed to support trade in patent rights. Both the courts and the U.S. Patent Office facilitated such transfers. And judges developed principles to protect the rights of all involved.

Patents as tradable assets were entirely unique to America's patent system. By 1880, eighty-five percent of American patents were licensed by their inventors. In England it was a mere thirty percent. It was the first time in the history of economics that an ordinary person, simply by applying reason, intelligence, and street smarts, could not only make a living as an inventor, but could become prosperous.

The impact of America's patent system on America's rise was staggering. There was a riot of innovation. As philosopher Andrew Bernstein captures it, "The 19th century in America was the single greatest era of technological and industrial advance in history." He points to such inventions as the reaper, the sewing machine, the telegraph, the airbrake for railroad cars. Later came the camera, the incandescent light bulb, the motion picture projector, the phonograph. Ripple effects triggered innovations in other sectors of the economy, such as, the revolution of transportation by automobile and airplane, and of manufacturing by mass production.[10]

Promethean Vision

If the inventive geniuses of the time are regarded as giants, the industrialists and business leaders were titans. This is the term reserved for the demigods of Greek literature, of whom Prometheus was one. To this day, *titan* is the term applied to such figures as Andrew Carnegie (Steel), John D. Rockefeller (Oil), James J. Hill (Railroads), J.P. Morgan (Banking and Finance). Contrary to the slur, "Robber Baron,"[11] each figure, in his own way and in his own field, personified Prometheus. Each had towering vision or *foresight*—the literal translation of the name "Prometheus."[12]

Vision was a defining characteristic of the age. The vision of the constitution's framers gave free rein to the focused vision of inventors, and these two forces—the framers and the inventors— provided the material infrastructure—the *capital*—for the towering vision of the business titans.

These three powers—framers, inventors, titans—were the catalysts for the greatest industrial growth in world history at a rate never witnessed before. Truly, they changed the face of America and justified the prescience of Thomas Paine. Truly they began the world over again. They were *empowered* to do so—and, without hesitation—did.[13]

It was the height of America's Industrial Revolution.

America's Rise -- Summary

How did America's constitution drive—power—her meteoric rise? The answer: the Founding Fathers framed the constitution in order to minimize initiated physical coercion or the threat thereof in human affairs. And equally important, they implicitly looked to limit government to a single function, that of protecting its citizens from those who would practice that evil. America's original constitution was a largely laissez-faire constitution, that is, a constitution largely in support of laissez-faire capitalism.

The declaration and constitution were truly revolutionary. Nothing like them, before or since, has ever been attempted. And because of them, America became the wealthiest and most powerful nation in history.

The Declaration of Independence unleashed the nation's inventive geniuses, entrepreneurs, and industrialists, freeing them to go where their vision—*guided by reason*—took them.

What made America's explosive rise possible? The answer in a word: Freedom.

AMERICA'S DECLINE

America's original "laissez-faire" constitution was an extraordinary achievement. But the constitution was not *explicitly* laissez-faire, and within a century of its ratification in 1787, omissions and loopholes started to erode its original laissez-faire character.

Major omissions include failures to explicitly banish initiated physical coercion or the threat thereof and to explicitly limit government to the sole function of protecting individual rights. *Loopholes* are the ambiguous, vague, open-to-interpretation expressions the Constitution contains, such as *public welfare, common good,* and *public interest.*

Economy

As a result of these constitutional flaws, the government's takeover of America's economy had started in earnest by the third quarter of the 19th century. A major event was the 1877 *Munn v Illinois* Supreme Court decision. Munn established the precedent that any property "clothed with a public interest" should be subject to government regulation and control. Thus, in one fell swoop, the Supreme Court effectively handed control of the American economy to the government.

"Public interest" embraced it all. That vague expression, ever open to interpretation, surely applies to any business property. That is exactly how the Supreme Court interpreted it in 1877.

And the precedent was set.

Munn was a major landmark and ominous harbinger of even greater assaults on economic freedom. Two laws in particular stand out: 1887's Interstate Commerce Act and 1890's Sherman Antitrust Act. Munn, Sherman, and Interstate Commerce were full frontal regulatory assaults marking the demise in America of what had been largely unfettered capitalism until then. The creation of the Federal

Reserve and the Sixteenth Amendment (Income Tax), both in 1913, clinched the demise.

There are many other programs, but these five alone are enough to dramatize the reality that, by the second quarter of the 20th century, coercive government had taken control of America's economy. Coercive regulation, as it inevitably does, multiplied ever since, in sync with an ever-growing income tax to fund it all.[14]

Why does regulation inevitably multiply? Several forces drive it. *Precedence* is one, as Munn illustrates. Any regulation sets the precedent for more regulation of the same kind. *Fiscal Constituencies* is another force. Large entitlement programs create huge voting blocks. These voting blocks are powerful forces which penalize any politician who would seek to roll back their entitlements. *Self-Perpetuation* is still another force. Most regulations ride into existence on the wings of "public interest" and "public welfare." Attempts to roll back regulations meet strident opposition from their advocates. The notions of "public interest" and the like almost always trump freedom.

Education

As with economics, America's regulatory takeover of education hijacked an already existing system which was largely private and successful.[15]

In the early colonies, private schools prevailed and provided an excellent education. This is not to say that all educators believed that private schools were the ideal. Educator Benjamin Rush is remembered for stating, "Let our pupil be taught that he does not belong to himself, but that he is public property"—this from a thinker who later signed the Declaration of Independence. Other views Rush articulated during his life were in the same vein. He was dead serious about the individual being *public property*. And he was not alone.

During the century following America's founding, major figures pushed for dramatic changes in education. Two such figures are Horace Mann (1796-1859) and John Dewey (1859-1952). Mann, as secretary of the Massachusetts Board of Education, founded the Common School Movement in 1837, ensuring that every child would receive a *public* education, funded by local taxes. And Dewey was the towering figure in American "Progressive" education which began in the 19th century and prevails to this day.

In his enormously influential book, *The School and Society,*[16] Dewey made it clear that all learning is ultimately for the purpose of "saturating him [the student] with the spirit of service." Schools should train children to fit into the social system rather than to think independently. Academic subjects should be watered down or outright replaced. Thus did Social Studies, for one example, replace the study of History. What little US history is taught is often, as philosopher Andrew Bernstein puts it, "leftist anti-American propaganda." He cites the example of a history written by Howard Zinn, a Marxist historian who was an active member of the Communist Party USA for years. Zinn's bestselling *People's History of the United States,*[17] Bernstein states, "is no more than a Communist slur against America." With two million copies sold, it is widely used in government schools.[18]

Bernstein notes that John Dewey's stature and erudition led to an army of progressive educators who were even more opposed to academic education than he was. William Heard Kilpatrick was one of them. Kilpatrick was a leading progressive educator of his time. From 1918 to 1940, he headed the Philosophy of Education department at Columbia University Teachers College. During those years, the Teachers College graduated more than thirty thousand educators from all states of the union, a large number of whom became America's education leaders. Columbia Teachers College under Kilpatrick became a super-spreader of progressive education in America.[19]

What is the legacy bequeathed to America by the above forces? Bernstein summarizes as follows: Today, nearly 90% of America's school children aged five through high school, go to public schools. Schools get their students by compulsory attendance laws—*force.* Typically, neither private school nor homeschooling is an affordable alternative for parents. The money taken from them in property taxes would help, but that money funds *public* education—a legacy of Horace Mann. Force rules throughout the government school system.

Bernstein, over a long career, has received a great many of America's government K-12 students into his college classrooms. He describes the academic performance of many students with a single word that speaks volumes: *"Heartbreaking."* [20]

Indoctrination has spread beyond K-12 to most public and so-called "private" colleges and universities, almost all of which are heavily dependent on funds from federal or state governments. Because of this financial dependence, these entities do not dare teach ideas or policies that conflict with those promulgated by government authorities.

Government Regulation Is Initiated Coercion

Government regulation is initiated physical coercion or the threat of it. And it is a threat which is ever present. Once established, a regulation is backed by the coercive power of government. Noncompliance is not an option unless one is willing to risk fines or arrest. Through regulation, government coercively molds what it believes to be good behavior. "We need to pass strong regulations," is how a Nobel laureate in economics put it, "embodying norms of good behavior, and appoint good regulators to enforce them."[21] This view is endemic in today's culture and is rarely challenged. Government coercion is simply accepted, like death and taxes, as the way things are.

On the above pages, we concentrated on Economics and Education. But government regulation is ubiquitous, whether it be in Science, Health Care, or any other enterprise.

America's Decline—In Essence

Just as America's phenomenal rise can be captured by a single concept, *Freedom,* America's decline can be captured by the single concept, *Coercion.* As we saw, the rise resulted from a largely laissez-faire constitution, and her decline resulted from the erosion of that constitution by coercive government intervention, ever intensifying to this day.[22]

A NEW BEGINNING

The state of today's America is not unique to America. Government coercion and the ever-present threat of it, is seen in all nations today, as a to-be-expected way of life.

Nations fall into two categories. Outright Dictatorship is one category, characterized by "one-party rule—executions without trial or with a mock trial, for political offenses—the nationalization or expropriation of private property—and censorship."[23] All other nations (the great majority) fall under a mixed category of freedom and controls.[24]

Never has there been a totally free nation. America, for the first and only time in history, came close, but ultimately, "close" was not good enough. The constitution, as discussed earlier, contained seeds of self-destruction: omissions and loopholes waiting to germinate. And finally, they did.

Is a New Beginning Possible?

Viewing the big picture, America's first century and a half marked her meteoric rise, to the freest and wealthiest nation in history; her second century and a half has marked her tragic decline, to that of—*not* a dictatorship—but that of a largely coercive regulatory state. Having explored how each happened, we can now offer a provisional answer to our all-important question:

Is the Vision of a permanent, totally

free sovereign nation truly possible

or is it ever to remain beyond our reach?

Were Thomas Paine alive today, his answer would likely be a qualified one: He would probably say "Yes," in light of the philosophy of Ayn Rand.[25] He would see that Rand's philosophy is vastly more powerful than what America's founders had in the late 18th century. And philosophy is what drives all the rest.

But he would caution that Real Estate and Defense are far greater challenges than they were three centuries ago. He would see that there exists no real estate in today's world, not even an island, which is not already under the sovereign control of some nation, with the exception of the polar regions.[26] Defense is equally challenging, given the reach and devastating firepower of modern weapon systems. Paine would be aware of these realities.

Can Philosophy alone address them? Clearly no—not directly. But indirectly, the answer could be Yes. Potentially, Rand's Objectivist philosophy could inspire the human and fiscal resources needed to take on the challenges of real estate and defense. And perhaps prevail over them.

Assuming that where the case, what might the vision of a totally-free sovereign state look like in the real world, that is, in actual physical reality?

Seasteading

The modern movement of Seasteading believes it answers that question. Futuristic artist renderings of the architecture, buildings, and interconnecting infrastructures of Seasteading projects are positively eye-popping. Clearly, they convey the spirit of beginning the world over again.[27]

Unfortunately, Seasteading,[28] (or its offshoots, such as Free Private Cities) involves forming a Special Economic Zone (SEZ) within a host nation.

But a host nation surrenders none of its sovereignty and does not take kindly to perceived threats to it. There is the grand vision of floating nations, beyond the sovereign borders of any country. But floating nations are prohibitively costly.[29]

How successful is Seasteading as the actualization of the vision of a permanent, totally free sovereign nation? Seasteading is actually a far cry from that vision. Seasteads receive concessions and permissions from a Host Nation but no sovereign status.[30] Nor do the leaders of the movement have a plan for changing that reality. Two of them, Joe Quirk and Patri Friedman simply state, "We have no specific, coherent vision of a better future to entice people with or to inflict on them."[31]

The Realm of Fiction

There exists only one place where the vision of a permanent, totally free sovereign nation has been actualized. That place is the human imagination, specifically the realm of fiction. Today's world seemingly poses insurmountable challenges to that vision, but the fiction writer works in the realm of "What Ifs," ideas waiting to be plucked, applied to the problems at hand as possible solutions, and then dramatized for the reader to consider as well.

Over the centuries a great body of utopian literature has devoted itself to new-beginning scenarios, starting with Plato's *Republic*.[32] In other literature it is more of a subtheme. Philosopher novelist Ayn Rand, for instance, in her 1957 novel, *Atlas Shrugged*, presents a character who ingeniously hastens the collapse of a self-destructing dystopian social system in order to clear the way for a new beginning.

In 2021, the authors of this essay published *The Prometheus Frontier*, a novel that imagines a new beginning by directly meeting the world's enormous challenges to that vision, despite the world's dystopian character.

Consider a few of the highlights: The protagonist, Marek Rankl, addresses Real Estate and Philosophy first, two of the greatest challenges. Rankl Marine Enterprises (RME) assumes ownership of a thousand square mile fictional island, Arete, from an aged and economically exhausted Caribbean dictator. Such an acquisition requires vast fiscal resources, and RME has those resources.

For Philosophy, Marek Rankl starts with a seminal founding document, a Declaration of Freedom which defines the Prometheus Frontier's basic philosophy. It is a philosophy which is to inspire and guide all other activities and then ensure the Frontier's long term survival and flourishing.

RME charters the Thomas Paine Society, two dozen RME associates with the ten year mission "to begin the world over again" by successfully addressing each remaining challenge. In the novel, we see this happen through the eyes of the protagonist's great grandson, Alek, who has arrived on Arete knowing nothing about it, but is taken through its evolution via a series of portals, flashbacks augmented by elements of science fiction.

Thus can fiction bring to life, in the human imagination, a fully functioning, flourishing, and free social system and then ensure its survival long term. Is this fictional scenario feasible in today's world? The balance of this essay addresses that question.

The Imperative of a New Place

We return now to the present day, to a world in which government repression of individual rights is seen in all nations. This has been true throughout history, which raises the question, Why?

In this essay, we focused on America's history to identify the answer. As we saw, her meteoric rise during the first century and a half after founding, was due to a largely laissez-faire constitution. And thus her decline to a nation in which rights are largely repressed stands out as all the more dramatic, visible, and therefore instructive. It contains three vital lessons.

Lesson One, a newly-founded nation needs to explicitly prohibit initiated physical coercion throughout the realm.

Lesson Two, at the same time, a newly-founded nation must make crystal clear that this prohibition applies to initiated coercion from any source, whether government or private, and that a proper government at any level (federal, state, local, or otherwise) uses force only in *retaliation* against those who have already initiated or threatened that evil.

Lesson Three, if a newly-founded nation fails to codify these prohibitions in its constitution, it will inevitably discover it has institutionalized an ***irreversibly*** repressive social system.

These three lessons, so vivid in America's history, are confirmed in the history of all nations. As we saw earlier, once established, repressive social systems are continually reinforced by the entrenched bureaucracies that led to them in the first place and are determined to keep them that way. That is, repressive social systems, once established, are ***irreversible***. They are like a ratchet wrench set to work in one direction only. If you attempt to reverse direction, the ratchet prevents it.

The implications of the three lessons are significant for the vision of beginning the world over again. Consider the realities: All nations without exception are repressive, and repressive social systems are irreversible once entrenched. As a result, if we are to begin the world over again with a fully free social system, we must have a new place. And properly formulated, our vision must have the following elements:

**A social system of pure Capitalism
starting life in a new place,
as a fully sovereign nation state.**

Is such a vision feasible in a world where government repression of individual rights is seen in all nations? Is it feasible in a world where the nation which has always been the greatest champion of individual rights, America, is in decline?

The Clarion Call

America's tragic decline in freedom, specifically in the freedom of its citizens from initiated government coercion, does not have to be a death knell. Sometimes it seems as if it could very well be leading to that. But America has been oscillating between periods of greater or lesser freedom for many decades, and we maintain that a more likely prognosis is that this oscillation will persist, despite those who believe the death knell for Western Civilization was sounded long ago.

Our conviction is that America's long-term decline is not a death knell but a clarion call. It is a clarion call for a great new beginning, in a new place that would evolve into something far greater than the last one, three centuries ago in late 18th century America.

America was the adopted nation of a towering intellect, a Russian immigrant, from whom we inherited a philosophy for beginning the world over again—again—and this time get it right. Her name is Ayn Rand. Her philosophy: Objectivism.

The role of our Declaration of Freedom, the new Frontier's philosophy, an application of Rand's philosophy, cannot be overemphasized. First, it explicitly avoids the constitutional loopholes and omissions critiqued in this essay under the heading "America's Decline." Second, the Founders of the new nation make the Declaration an integral part of the Frontier's new Constitution by making it the Preamble. Third, Article One, Section One of the Constitution's body will explicitly articulate the "Primacy of the Declaration of Freedom Principle." This principle mandates that all Constitutional articles, clauses, and amendments, in perpetuity, will be fully consistent with the Preamble. For the full text of the Declaration of Freedom, in three parts, see the Appendix.

We are immensely fortunate to be living in this era, with the potential of a new beginning before us, ever beckoning. Beginning the world over again—again—the vision promoted in this essay, could be a long time in coming. Conceivably, it could start on America's island territory of Puerto Rico, politically reconfigured as our "new place" (think Hong Kong and its 99-year lease). Or some other part of the world at large.

But whatever locus the new beginning or "place" takes, and no matter the challenges, it will surely have Americans behind it, to nurture, support, and inspire. And ensure its flourishing in perpetuity.[34]

Paving the Way

Great challenges face any vision of beginning the world over again, especially when it is to be based on the philosophy of Objectivism. They are working on incremental change, they are *not* working on overcoming the challenges of starting over.

All the organizations working for incremental change and improvement help to pave the way for a new start by forestalling the total collapse of Western Civilization. There is the *Prometheus Foundation,* the *Objective Standard Institute*, the *Ayn Rand Institute,* the *American Capitalist Party*, the *Atlas Society.* And there are others outside the Objectivist orbit, like the Foundation for Economic Education and the Mises Institute, each of them focused on bringing about a Capitalist social system. And each is working to prepare the world by targeting a specific portion of that world, whether a large population or small. Oftentimes, they target the same audiences, with different material, or emphases.

There is also a pronounced division of labor. There are Objectivist intellectuals "laboring" in the field of education, historical analysis, energy policy, and so on. Others still, such as those who founded the American Capitalist Party, are engaging the political realm. Yes, it is to be expected that a natural division of labor is evident in the many organizations looking to actualize the vision of a social system of pure Capitalism.[35]

Enter the unique *Thomas Paine Institute (TPI),* the latest addition to the freedom movement.

THE THOMAS PAINE INSTITUTE

The Thomas Paine Institute: A Division of Labor

The Thomas Paine Institute (TPI) is a think tank, with leaders who are in full agreement with the Objectivist philosophy of Ayn Rand. It invites all Objectivists and active minded non-Objectivists to share its vision and become TPI members.

Uniqueness

TPI's uniqueness—setting it apart from all other Objectivist initiatives—is twofold.

First, it is unique in its vision of what a new beginning would entail, namely, a social system of pure Capitalism, to be given birth, from its inception, in a new place, and inaugurated as a fully independent sovereign nation state.

Second, it is unique in being solely focused on the challenges that must be overcome to actualize that vision in the world of today.

Immediate Goal: Build a Following

TPI is committed to a soaring vision: a social system of pure Capitalism to be given birth in a new place and inaugurated as an independent sovereign nation state.

But bringing a vision like this into concrete physical reality requires that we begin at the beginning. It takes talented intellectuals. And thus, do we seek colleagues in spirit who enjoy great challenges and are willing to commit time to meeting them. We discussed those challenges in the above pages. Although they are great, they are not insurmountable.

Intermediate Goals

Write a new constitution modeled after the US Constitution that incorporates our Declaration of Freedom as an integral part of the constitution in perpetuity.

Mobilize our resources to establish a Strategic Administrative Region (like Hong Kong), but using a new Constitution with our Declaration of Freedom.

What TPI Offers

We, the founders of TPI, now repeat, once again, Thomas Paine's call late in the eighteenth century, with the addition of one word: We have it in our power to begin the world over again—*again*.

What do we have to offer? We offer the same soaring value that the original Thomas Paine offered. We offer the promise of a new beginning. And along with it, we offer the unmatched exhilaration of working toward it over time.

The above pages give you key details of the work needed. Perhaps our sense of urgency has become your own. We invite you to share your thoughts with us.

Imagine a role at TPI beckoning to you, yours for the taking.

Public Relations

The public relations team will promote TPI's vision with other freedom-loving organizations, newsletters, and magazines. The public relations team will generate articles and white papers to promote TPI.

TPI's Political Position

Our political position is set forth in our Declaration of Freedom, in which we advance the vital importance of government for a free society to exist and flourish. In other words, we disavow anarchists and anarcho-capitalists.

Administration

The initial organization of the Thomas Paine Institute will include a Board of Directors, an Executive Director, and Research Staff.

Board of Directors: The Board of Directors will set the strategic direction, oversees finances, and will ensure the organization fulfills its mission. We are seeking board members who support the vision of the Thomas Paine Institute to begin the world over again.

Executive Director: The Executive Director will lead the day-to-day operations, implementing the board's vision and managing staff.

Research Staff: The research staff will conduct research, produce reports and policy recommendations. We are seeking volunteers with expertise in specific fields like real estate, defense, finance, human resources, philosophy, law, and computer hardware and software technology.

***

Philosopher Andrew Berstein captures well the ever-present driving forces which will make it happen.

> ***The human capacity to reason and the yearning for freedom and prosperity, will survive as long as humanity itself; no degree of irrational philosophy or repressive government will suffice to stamp these out.*** [36]

****

APPENDIX: DECLARATION OF FREEDOM

Declaration of Freedom

Preamble for the Constitution of [Name]

This Declaration of Freedom is adapted by Alex Bleier, Jerrold Meyer, and Kevin Osborne, from <u>The Prometheus Frontier</u>, the novel, Copyright ©2021.

FOUNDATIONAL TRUTHS

When in the course of human events, the nation that was once the freest the world has ever seen, whose government— a Constitutional Republic—was the first and only one in history explicitly founded on the moral principle of individual rights—when that nation, for centuries the sole beacon for the world's oppressed—when that nation itself loses sight of what it means to be free and, instead, makes initiated physical coercion and the violation of individual rights a way of life—it is then necessary to restart freedom in a new place.

We the men and women of [Name] hereby announce that we have given birth to such a place and proudly advance this declaration of freedom—freedom from initiated physical coercion— as its seminal founding document.

We hold certain fundamental truths to be observable and inducible facts of reality:

— *that all individuals are born equal in their possession of reason, the distinguishing faculty elevating them above all other creatures,*

— *that individual human life—the ultimate value and standard of the good—in order to survive and to flourish, requires the free exercise of our faculty of reason. For, unlike all other creatures, humans have no automatic knowledge of how to survive. Humans must use reason,*

— *that the initiation of physical coercion, because it abrogates the free exercise of reason and thereby human life, must be abolished from all human affairs,*

— *that standing in opposition to this evil are individual rights, which all men and women possess, the most fundamental of which are life, liberty, property, and the pursuit of happiness,*

— *that the absolute, objective basis of rights is not an alleged supreme being or social group or government but the immutable requirements for an individual human life to survive and flourish in a social context,*

— *that a constitutionally controlled government is nonetheless an absolute necessity, strictly limited to the sole sacred purpose of securing and protecting individual rights against initiated physical coercion,*

— *that such a government equally protects all men and women against such coercion and itself uses force only in retaliation against those who have initiated that evil or have threatened to do so.*

THE CASE FOR A NEW START

But when government itself makes it a practice to initiate physical coercion, or to legalize its initiation by others, it defaults on its sole sacred function which is to protect its citizens from initiated force. We declare that throughout the world, governments exhibit this evil. Respect for reason demands that we set forth the evidence. To wit:

— Throughout the world, nations pay lip service to rights in their constitutions, but then permit groups, even their own governments, to take them as sanctions to violate individual rights. This corrupts the meaning of rights which, when correctly understood, are possessed only by individuals.

— Rights are moral sanctions for individual action in a social context. Correctly induced, rights protect the individual from the group, especially that largest and most powerful of groups— government. Yet throughout the world, all governments have institutionalized the violation of the individual rights of their citizens.

— Property rights mean that individuals have the right to dispose of the product of their labor, or their earnings from it, as they see fit, providing they do not infringe or threaten the rights of others. Property rights protect individuals from slavery—slavery in any part of their lives, or in any portion. Property rights are moral sanctions for individuals to seek, gain, and dispose of the product of their work—not sanctions for some group to expropriate and dispose of it. Yet, throughout today's world, throughout history, that evil is seen.

— In all the world's nations, debased governments, and the groups they enable, regulate all sectors of their country's life, including, in many nations, matters of religion or conscience. In developed nations, endemic public-private-sector cronyism produces corruption, coercive monopolies, and legalized plunder. Vast fiscal constituencies require countless government

agencies and ever mounting debt. Cradle-to-grave dependence on government makes self-reliance—once a matter of cultural pride in more enlightened nations—a lost virtue. Pillaging by rampant pressure group warfare enervates entire cultures. Throughout the world, these depredations are seen.

— We support efforts to roll back repressive regulations. But repressive social systems are continually reinforced by the entrenched bureaucracies that led to them in the first place and are determined to keep them that way. For this and other reasons, repressive socioeconomic systems, once entrenched, are virtually irreversible. Attempts to effect change with incremental improvement can help to control damage and alleviate human suffering but cannot bring about lasting change. History has always demonstrated this.

We declare that if political freedom is the goal, that is, freedom from initiated coercion, then the world's populations have only one course of action. That course is to start over in new places, from scratch, with constitutions banishing the initiation of force throughout the realm, including the most common source of initiated force, that from government against its citizens. This course is what our new nation, [Name], is taking, and this Declaration of Freedom is the preamble of [New Nation's] constitution.

PURE CAPITALISM: [NAME'S] SOCIOECONOMIC SYSTEM

We, the founders of [New Nation] proudly proclaim this Declaration of Freedom and renounce initiated physical coercion. Indeed, our socioeconomic system utterly outlaws it. Our social system enables all human interactions, with no exception, to take place through voluntary persuasion and trade by the free exercise of reason. This is what pure capitalism is:

To Begin the World Over Again

"Capitalism is a social system based on the recognition of individual rights, including property rights, in which all property is privately owned."

We proclaim that Capitalism is, and always shall be, the socioeconomic system of [New Nation].

Under [New Nation's] system of pure Capitalism, the Constitution, for which this declaration is the preamble, prohibits the government, at any level, from intervention into finance, economy, education, medicine, science, religion, or any other activity or enterprise, including those yet to be developed.

We recognize that as long as human nature is volitional, certain forces from within and without will initiate and threaten physical coercion. But our government exists to execute a sole sacred function. [New Nation's] government addresses physical force initiated from within by a legal system of police and courts. It addresses physical force initiated from without by a virtually impregnable system of defense. And [New Nation] will not want for impassioned citizens and allies to defend freedom, with enlightened professionals leading the way on the intellectual and military ramparts.

As we set out on this grand endeavor, we the leaders of [New Nation] proudly adopt an exalted oath uttered long ago by the founders of the nation to which we alluded at the opening of this declaration. It is fitting that we adopt their oath as our own, for the inspiration of their original founding is timeless.

We mutually pledge to each other our Lives, our Fortunes and our sacred Honor.

With these words ringing down through the ages, we know that all men and women of good will on Earth—East and West—will join us in our quest—our quest for a new Age of Reason—our quest to begin the world over again, with the birth of a new Enlightenment.

SIGNATURES:

____

To follow the work of the Thomas Paine Institute or to join our efforts, write to us and join our mailing list at: info@thomaspaineinstitute.com

ENDNOTES

[1] "Common Sense," Pamphlet first published January 1776, W.&T. Brandford, Philadelphia PA, Subject III, "Thoughts on the present state of American affairs," opening sentence.

[2] See "Common Sense," Subject IV "Of the Present Ability of America."

[3] "Common Sense," Subject IV.

[4] "Common Sense," Subject IV.

[5] Professor C. Bradley Thompson, in *America's Revolutionary Mind*, (New York: Encounter Books, 2019) argues that the concepts of a free society based on individual rights had already taken hold in the minds of the majority of the colonists before the armed revolution. In contradistinction, the French Revolution and the Polish revolutions failed due to the absence of rights-based thinking in the minds of the majority of people in those countries.

[6] See Michael Dahlen, "The Rise of American Big Government: A Brief History of How We Got Here," *The Objective Standard*, Vol. 4, No. 3, Fall 2009.

[7] Henry R. Nothhaft with David Kline, *Great Again: revitalizing America's entrepreneurial leadership*, (Boston: Harvard Business Review Press, 2011), 70.

[8] Nothhaft & Kline, 71.

[9] Naomi R. Lamoreaux and Kenneth L. Sokoloff, editors, *Financing Innovation in the United States, 1870 to the Present*, (Cambridge, Massachusetts: The MIT Press, 2007), 4

[10] Andrew Bernstein, *Capitalist Manifesto*, (Lantham, Maryland: University Press of America, 2005), 138.

[11] The "Robber Baron" slur is often leveled against the productive geniuses of America's Industrial Revolution by Anti-Capitalist historians. Bernstein, in his *Capitalist Manifesto*, exhaustively counters this insidious perversion of history in a 44 page Appendix, 395-438, titled "Robber Barons or Productive Geniuses," supplemented with three pages of bibliographic notes, 469-472.

[12] Kevin Osborne, *The Prometheus Connection*, (Mutekikon Publications, 2014), chapters 1 and 2

[13] For a luminous account of this period from a philosophic standpoint, see Leonard Peikoff, *The Ominous Parallels*, (New York, Stein and Day, 1982), Ch5 "The Nation of the Enlightenment."

[14] See again Michael Dahlen, "The Rise of American Big Government: A Brief History of How We Got Here."

[15] Andrew Bernstein, *Why Johnny Still Can't Read or Write or Understand Math And What We Can Do About It,* (New York, Nashville, Bombadier Books, 2022) Chapter 2 "Superb Education in America's Past."

[16] This book which began life as a series of lectures was first published in 1899 in book form.

[17] HarperCollins (New York: 1980), 1st edition.

[18] Bernstein, 77-78.

[19] Bernstein, 36-41.

[20] Bernstein, xvi-xviii.

[21] Joseph E. Stiglitz, "In No One We Trust," a December 21, 2013 excerpt from *The Great Divide*, a series on inequality in the New York Times.

[22] For a moral component of this tragedy, see Andrew Bernstein "Capitalism in One Lesson: Capitalism Is the Only Practical System Because It Is the Only Moral System," The Objective Standard, Vol. 19, No. 1, Spring 2024.

[23] Ayn Rand, *The Virtue of Selfishness,* "Collectivized 'Rights'" (New York: Signet Paperback, 1964), 105.

[24] Ayn Rand referred to these nations as "Mixed Economies" and wrote about them at length. See *The Ayn Rand Lexicon,* compiled by Harry Binswanger, (New York: New American Library, 1988) available as a free download at https://courses.aynrand.org/lexicon/. Select "Lexicon" and go to "Mixed Economy."

[25] For the most comprehensive single reference, see Leonard Peikoff, *Objectivism: The Philosophy of Ayn Rand,* (New York: Dutton Penguin, 1991).

[26] There is no single country owning either of the polar regions. For the Arctic, see https://en.wikipedia.org/wiki/Territorial_claims_in_the_Arctic. For the Antarctic, see The Antarctic Treaty system https://en.wikipedia.org/wiki/Antarctic_Treaty_System.

[27] Joe Quirk with Patri Friedman, *Seasteading*: how floating nations will restore the environment, enrich the poor, cure the sick, and liberate humanity from politicians, (New York: Free Press Simon & Schuster, 2017).

[28] In this essay, unless otherwise indicated the term *Seasteading* applies to its offshoots as well.

[29] See Quirk & Friedman, *Seasteading*, 8 pages of illustrations starting at 145.

[30] For a clear presentation of the dynamics of these relationships, see Titus Gebel's white paper, "Free Private Cities – A New Operating System for Living Together," January 2023 v2.0. https://free-cities.org/wp-content/uploads/2023/06/Whitepaper-Free-Private-Cities-A-New-Operating-System-for-Living-Together.pdf."

[31] Quirk and Friedman, 31.

[32] See https://en.wikipedia.org/wiki/Utopia.

[33] See Osborne, *The Prometheus Connection*.

[34] The Epilogue of *The Prometheus Frontier* novel imagines a scenario resulting from the catalytic effect a successful new beginning would trigger, as follows: "The renown of the Prometheus Frontier leads many of the world's islands to join its federation of islands. On Earth's continents, metaphorical islands form as well. Regions and towns, or states and provinces seeking to live by the Frontier's Declaration of Freedom--its philosophy, its *spirit*--become virtual islands of freedom. The Paine Society ever pursues the vision that, with enough of these virtual islands in place, conceivably even earth's advanced and largely coercive nations could '*begin the world over again*' and become part of the Prometheus Frontier."

[35] As with "Mixed Economy," Ayn Rand wrote about pure Capitalism extensively during her life. See The Ayn Rand Lexicon (https://courses.aynrand.org/lexicon/), this time for excerpts from her many essays on "Capitalism."

[36] Bernstein, *Capitalist Manifesto*, 394.

[37] See Ayn Rand's 1963 essay "Man's Rights" that appeared in her books, The Virtue of Selfishness (1964), Capitalism the Unknown Ideal (1967), and elsewhere.

[38] See Ayn Rand's 1963 essay, "The Nature of Government" in her books, The Virtue of Selfishness (1964), Capitalism the Unknown Ideal (1967), and elsewhere.

www.ingramcontent.com/pod-product-compliance
Lightning Source LLC
Chambersburg PA
CBHW070754260726
48660CB00007B/3118